To Alex —
May poetry's power
grace all the seasons
of your life.

Florence McGinn
May, 2005

Blood Trail

Blood Trail

Poems by Florence McGinn

Introduction by Victor di Suvero

PENNYWHISTLE PRESS

Edited by: Victor di Suvero
Typesetting: Katherine Forrest
Cover Design: Ted Slampyak
Cover Art: *Landscape in the Manner of Li T'ang,* Ch'iu Ying
Permission Number FG4295. Courtesy of Freer Gallery of Art
Rights & Reproductions, Freer Sacker Lock Box, Dept. 0604
Washington DC 20073-0604
Photograph: Bob Warren
Typeface: Caslon and New Berolina

Library of Congress Card Catalog Number: 97-075994
ISBN: 0-938631-34-9 paper

Blood Trail is the first full-length collection from Chinese-American poet Florence McGinn.

Early on, we encounter *"Speaking the Language,"* a tribute to her experience as a child adjusting to a new country. This theme of adjustment—*change*—is evident in nearly every poem. The collection moves forward through her life in four sections, touching on the subjects of the power of the feminine ("Paths of Blood"), and later, reflections on familial connection and mortality ("For the Dead").

A lauded high school English teacher in New Jersey, McGinn's poetry has appeared in such literary journals as *Eclectic Literary Forum, Midwest Poetry Review, Modern Haiku,* and *Cicada. Blood Trail* offers insight into her world as a Chinese-American, a mother, a woman, and—perhaps most importantly—as a poet.

Acknowledgments

Grateful acknowledgment is made to the following periodicals in which some of the poems in this collection first appeared, often in an earlier form.

Creative Woman: "Spring Planting with my Daughter," "Nine Months"
Eclectic Literary Forum: "Holding the Words"
Footworks: Paterson Literary Review: "Two Left Paradise"
New Jersey Review of Literature: "Messages"
Parnassus Literary Journal: "On Writing"
Poet's Pen: reprint of "Nine Months"
The River: "Guidance"
Sage Woman: "Inside the Poetry"
Women's Work: "Meal for the Ancestors"
Writing for Our Lives: "Choices," "Long Illness"

Grateful acknowledgment is made to the following haiku periodicals in which some of the haiku in this collection first appeared, sometimes in an earlier form.

Bear Creek Haiku: "on your lips"
Cicada: "my breasts rise" Best of Issue Award, "your sleeve corner"
Frogpond: "silent, dawn flight"
Haiku Headlines: "your fragrant scent"
Modern Haiku: "graveled breathing," "fragrance"

Cover Photograph by Bob Warren

I acknowledge with grateful love my husband, Joseph, as well as my daughter and son, Nerissa and Brion, for their unique love, support, and reading.
I thank my sister, Nancy Bjerke, for her support and reading.

I would like to thank Hunterdon Central Regional High School and Sarnoff Corporation for sabbatical grants for Dr. McGinn and myself which permitted a year's sabbatical in California. I sincerely acknowledge the quiet influences of Brian Glennon, Dan VanAntwerp, and John Smith. I thank Dr. Michael Mahon of California State University for insightful mentorship as well as Dr. Lyle Smith and Dr. Noreen Larinde of California State University for their readings. I sincerely acknowledge Linda Batz, Dr. Roland Pare, Dr. Judy Gray, Raymond Farley, Dr. Frank DeCavalcante, and Dr. William Fernekes for their support.

Inspiration and support come from many sources. I sincerely acknowledge students Chris Dymek, Tim Gorton, Dan DiMicco, Kate Lynch, Richard Morrison, Robert Zaino, Douglas Gorton, Emily Judson, Neela Mookerjee, and Sujay Pandit.

For Joseph

Contents

Sources

Moments

Tracks

Living Trail

NOTE: ➡ *this mark indicates the poem continues on the following page.*

Introduction by Victor di Suvero

The cross-cultural currents that have enriched American writing in
the latter part of the 20th century continue to be part of the literary
scene today. From Amy Tan's **Joy Luck Club** to the rich variety of
Maya Angelou's African-American sensibility, the reading public
has had the opportunity to experience feelings and conditions more
varied than at any other time in American literary life.

Florence McGinn's work continues that cross-cultural adventure.
Her poetry, crafted with care for the detail of her Chinese heritage,
reaches into our consciousness with current American scenes and
with language that touches our hearts.

The shorter, personal poems in the series entitled "Moments"
evoke the ideogram of Chinese writing. Thoughts and feelings are
juxtaposed with an economy of language that evokes the reader in
ways that more detailed, expanded verse will not. Grounded in the
tradition of Japanese haiku, these short poems are kin also to the
early Tang poems of McGinn's heritage.

As a Chinese-American married to an Irish-American scientist,
teaching in American public schools where her grace, care, and talent
have been recognized nationally, Florence McGinn's sensibilities as
expressed in her poems about family life, about relationships, about
parenting are all infused with the variety of her cultural heritage
combined with American challenges she faces in today's world.

Her grandmother, dying, remembers "the drifting dust of a Canton
village street waiting to turn to thick, sucking mud when summer
skies flowed over" in a poem that ends "with farewells, but pregnant
with clear birthing waters." It is this sort of juxtaposition that is
continuously used to create the tension that makes the poems in
Blood Trail sing.

It would be easy to say that the subjects of so many of the poems are
universal and the feelings expressed could belong to any one culture or
another. However, just as with the culinary arts, the art of poetry is

grounded in the cultural experience of the poet as well as that of the poet's audience. Here we have a rare example of specific cultural and historical references that are Chinese worked into the current American idiom so skillfully that the reader is taken to that place of recognition which transcends origins and consequently makes the experience of the poem his or her own.

It has been said that love and poetry are the only two countries where, when visited, the rest of the world disappears. McGinn's poems are of that kind. The involvement of the person reading them excludes all other sensibilities, and the reader's involvement is total.

In her poem "Speaking the Language" she summarizes her experience in becoming proficient in a language other than the one she was born into. Her clarity transports the reader. All the spoken and unspoken feelings about learning English, her family's involvement in her learning process result in an understanding of the bridges crossed when one's language changes or is changed.

The poems in this collection can be defined as singular contributions to and evidence of the American dream working. With dedication, grace, and persistence, a voice speaks truths, reaffirming that the human condition is one that we all share, that making love and celebrating it is an appropriate function for us all, that working from one set of values to another can be a process of enrichment rather than denial, and that a worthwhile future can be shaped out of a difficult past.

Florence McGinn is not afraid to tackle difficult issues in her work and in her personal life. The evidence is in the poems themselves, growing up, becoming a woman, loving and parenting. Looking both to her past as daughter and to her present as mother, she takes us through the changing qualities of a life lived fully and responsibly and shares her experiences with practical and caring grace.

Sources

Respect For the Dragon

Mother's oldest brother brought China
with him like a dragon's fierce shadow
sewn to the heels of his black slippers.
He carried that gleaming, basalt shadow
coast to coast, from San Francisco
to the concrete alleys of Brooklyn.
In his arms and heart, he carried
his little sister, my mother.

Although I am Elder Daughter,
I do not carry Uncle's dragon fire.
It has been diluted because I did not
believe in it, fizzled and faded
when I clapped my hands for Tinkerbell.

But I watch my mother
keep tradition with a deftness
like the quick sealing of a won ton.
While others' memories
wash clean like the swirling
of white rice before steaming,
Mother remembers in the watering
of white peonies, the Tai Chi stretch
Uncle showed her against arthritis pain,
the fragrant, pork broth scent
of her kitchen, and her murmured
Chinese prayers for Uncle's soul.

And I hear from Mother's smallest
movements, like the peeling
of a fresh tangerine, an ancient,
winged language of metaphors built
on an inner syntax matching my own.

Uncle, little sister casts a dragon's shadow.

First Son

Grandfather rubs black hair
on my new brother's tiny head.
"First son's first son. Good fortune."

I lean against Grandfather's leg
reaching, pushing for the baby.
He presses my hands away.

Mother gathers me into her lap
as eager men shoulder around,
large hands on brother's rich, wild hair.

Grandmother picks up a steamed dumpling
and dips its glistening whiteness
into dark soy sauce and smiles to me.

I open my mouth to shrimp's
rich juices, soy's salty tang.
I bite to its hot, firm center.

Brother cries, naked, in that circle.
Forehead pinched, ears pressed,
belly prodded, legs and arms pulled.

"Money here."   *"Lucky ears."*
"Smart. A doctor, a lawyer, maybe."
"Pride, pride of his ancestors."

Later, I hold baby brother.
I blow softly on hair, dark
as a raven's glistening feathers.

I press my cheek to its black silk,
blue-black as inkberries
washed in midnight rain.

I fall asleep, holding baby brother,
foolishly believing his hair,
so soft and dark, would never change.

Speaking the Language

For a long time,
my Cantonese family
was the only Chinese family in town.
I spoke English well,
but my tiny Asian face stopped conversations.
Adults encountered would say single words
and mime simple actions
like smiling, gesticulating actors
in a silent street show.

I would watch,
and I would not speak.

Jostling currents of adults
would move around me,
touching me softly
as the stream flows past
young cattails willing to bend.
I saw others, my age, shriek and object,
impinge and demand incessantly
as the nestling calls to its vagrant parents.
I did not know their tricks.
I kept a shy, intent vigil to gain their knowledge.
Watching in silence became an accustomed joy
When I entered kindergarten,
the teacher called my mother.
I did not know she had come to school
during the quiet walk to the principal's office,
holding my teacher's unresponsive hand.
I listened. My problem
was carefully explained.
We are not sure what to do
because your daughter cannot
speak English.

My mother's eyes, the color of brown silt
in a still pond, looked long at me.
She asked the anxious administrator
how they knew I could not speak their language.

She watches everything attentively,
but she has not spoken one word
all week.

My eyes
as surely as a frightened, shrieked
protest exploding in the air
told my mother
they had not asked me.

My mother turned
to the waiting officials.
She spoke low in soft apology.
I hung my head as she said
I spoke a little English.
I wanted to flutter forward
to speak English in the fluency I used
with comfortable ease at home,
but her bowed head stopped me.
My mother indicated the family's mistake;
we would speak only English at home now,
so the children would learn
and speak with no accent.
The children would not have her accent,
and I, the oldest, would learn quickly.
They would be surprised at the pace
of my learning in such a good school.
She promised that.

I stand in front of my own English classroom now.
Faces turn toward me in eagerness
as I read favorite, brimming lines
from Merwin, Yeats, Kinnell.
My English is clear and precise, unaccented.

Yet, there are long, desert dry moments
when my tongue stalls and aches
for the graceful rise and fall,
the drawn out vowels,
of my childhood chatter,
my forgotten, family language.

Laundry Woman

Visiting Grandmother's laundry,
I watched her hands grasp
the hot iron and sweep across
white shirts with silent speed.
I would smell fresh soap
and damp starch and listen
to the door's jangling bell
as each customer entered.

Brooklyn was washed
and starched in her hands.

Today, Grandmother's
hands shake, unable
to encircle nine decades.
She cannot wash
large-knuckled fingers
herself. She does not
remember how
to comb her hair.

When Father enters
her bedroom, she calls
him by a brother's name.
He answers
without pause.

➡

Father says she wants
to rise out of bed
and walk outdoors,
but I do not see
Grandmother with
a straight spine,
shopping bags
slapping hard
against her calves.

My grandmother cannot
struggle upright
to grasp her bed's
cold metal railings.

When Mother powders
Grandmother's arms
and creams her face
and age-spotted hands,
I try hard to remember
the scent of soap and starch.

Inescapable

One hand pressed against the dining room table's
dark mahogany surface. Summer mornings
stacked stiffly like unscraped dinner dishes
as Mother gracefully brushed Chinese characters
for me to study. She laughed at my awkward
strokes and left me to copy phrases and songs.
The sun streamed through white curtains, the cat
stretched on the porch until the German Shepherd
bounded up the steps. He cocked his head
and barked as I spoke my Chinese words.
Mother heard, of course, and told me,
"No bicycle rides until after Chinese lessons!"
My dog waited as I stroked figures like leaf veins
down and up, left to right across sheets
of white paper. *"No short cuts! Better not
let your mother-in-law see you write so poorly!"*
I was nine, and I believed. *"Who will marry you,
you write like that."*   Mother shook her head
as she put away our ink and brushes.
"Not too much sun." She touched
my skin to see if I was still marriageable
or wrinkled into shameful toughness
by careless sun. *"Softball! It will make
your knuckles big."*   She checked
my hands to see if any sport had abused them,
shook her head at the folly of American gym classes.
But when report cards came, she frowned
at the Pass written next to Physical Education,
tapped the spot with an accusing finger, and asked,
"Why not an A here, too?"   Explanations
never helped. So I waited for her to sign
the report card and put it into my lunch box.

➡

On my own, I pedaled my bicycle,
pumping furiously, and the dog raced
beside me as my wheels spun up grass or dirt.
I left behind the ginger and oil scents
of Mother's kitchen, the taste of bitter teas brewed
to ward off anticipated chills, and the anxious
imperatives of duty. I tried not to hear
my family's iron whisper like steam rising
from an ancient skillet, *"Tradition."* A part
of me sizzled away. *"Blood. Obedience."*
The scent of dissipating self was a familiar one.
I rode far from the farm house and lay
alone near fields of soybean or hay, but always,
always, stretched out in thick, sun-screening shade.

Childhood Tremors

Steep, wooden steps lead
down to the adult world of the kitchen
bathed in night shadows and stark light.
Night vibrates with anger
taut in hoarse, parental shouts.
Inner earthquake tremors
modulate to linguistic rhythms
of Cantonese interrupted with English.

Awakened from sleep's warmth,
my sister and I press against each other
in searching movements down the hall.
Our feet grow cold as our backs
press hard against old walls.
I move closer toward the bottom steps.

When I come to the window,
I pause as a dense silence
saturates night air.
I look outward to see shadows cast
by our climbing tree's branches
bathed by kitchen light.
A forgotten doll with a frozen smile,
weary of childish pommeling,
leans with patience
against the broad base
of that maple's thick trunk.

I hear a soft swallow and look
up steep, uncarpeted stairs.
Little Sister sits silently
with her arms around her knees.

➡

Sister's small hand fills mine
as we shuffle back to our rooms.
I pause at her door until mattress spring
sounds are replaced with the winged
whistle of the hunting owl.

Darkness in my room quivers
with questions. I reach for a book
as I switch on my bedside lamp.
Tiny cracks of earthquake movements,
my insistent fears, appear upon the walls.
I brace myself with the fibrous strength
of family order, gird myself
in the being of Oldest Sister.

Delivering Death

Summer whisks fingers
translucent with shimmering heat
across the blue whir of dragonfly wings.
Algae floats thickly upon pond water
like long hair twisted into knots of scum.
Two does step into mud, lower their heads,
and alternately drink and snort.

It is a sound, almost human,
in an inhuman time
of humid weight and fiery air.

The buzz of gnats and black flies,
loud like a wheezing engine,
draws me away from the pond edge.

Insects swarm and rise above
the farm road's ditch and coarse weeds.
A young rabbit, its back legs torn and twisted,

lies visible from the road. As I stare, it lifts
its head, eyes covered with flies, and cries
a thin, high wail. I shudder and back away.

When I find the large rock and lift its weight
with both hands, I flinch. I want to offer
comfort and can bring only release.

I cannot go near. I find instead a thick stick.
I plan one, swift stroke, but I swing
and slam five, maybe six, times. It is hard

to stop. I run and heave the stick deep
into the still pond. I keep on running
from the dead rabbit and from myself.

Facing the Secrets

The Chinese were masters at locking up secrets.   *Nothing is wrong*
with uncle.   I knew not to ask why uncle could not read,
could not add or subtract. I would not question why
he could only go as far down the block as a child. It was strange
because uncle, a grown man, was treated like a child, like a woman
without a real role.   *China Man 'tard* was what I heard outside
Grandparents' laundry door.   *Uncle used to be so smart*
was all Mother whispered.   I determined to make no peace
with darkness. I became a tiny diviner of secrets, a breaker of locks.

Eventually, no one had to explain why   why the men never smoked
or drank with him   why he would go to their cars, only to watch
them drive off without acknowledging his presence. Grandmother
would come out and lead him back into the laundry, feed him dim sum,
treat him like the little boy he would always be.   I was only halfway
to the secret held in communal darkness.   Death unlocked its fetters.

What a temper Grandfather had!   Whiskey glasses tilted in ancestral honor
of a patriarch I remembered only as stern. I objected. I had not seen
Grandfather lose his temper, never seen him shout.   The first time
I spoke it was like a dragon had lifted its head. Dragon smoke obscured
the room with its sizzling tension. All eyes turned to my father, the oldest son.
His jaw stiffened before he spoke. *Go to your room. Do schoolwork.*

Even the best locks grew rusty with time. I waited.   It was several years,
and I asked the women instead. Auntie's eyes never left mine, but I sensed
shifting within dark corridors. Grandfather's death and time had reduced
barriers but not to insignificance.   Again, I waited.   *The large machines*
in the back room of the laundry, do you remember them? Grandfather prevented
me from going there alone, but I tried to recall washers, dryers, tubs, and wringers.

➡

Auntie began to wash dirt from bok choy stems, so I nodded to win her back. She wiped her hands on her apron. She sat, back stiff, before speaking. *Back then, Grandfather's authority was final. He punished as he saw fit. After Grandmother took little uncle out of the machine, he was not the same. Nothing was the same.* Each woman watched me, and no face was turned aside. saw shades of futility and clenched jaws of anguished acceptance. Nothing could be changed. I saw stubborn strength and unburied anger. No forgiveness was offered on any woman's face.

Adult female relatives watched horror break the final locks. *Your father became eldest son then.* When Mother stood up, Auntie began to chop bok choy. Mother counted rice bowls carefully before she spoke in a voice like a clicking lock. You understand now. Mother began to rinse dark water from black mushrooms.

I placed wooden chopsticks by porcelain bowls rounded with steaming rice. The scer of peanut oil, ginger, and garlic grew fragrant. Sizzling filled the air. I walked aw to stand in the darkened living room. Mother and Auntie watched but did not stop n The sounds of eating rose and faded. I remembered Grandmother's voice. *No use to complain. Watch the sunset. Watch the sunrise. You see, every day the sun learns to make peace with night's dark.* Grandmother, your secret, tell me how.

Messages

One photograph corner is ripped away,
and someone once folded this album page,
but I hold this bit of time, before my time,
and stare long into the eyes, the frozen smiles,
of a formal family portrait.

Grandfather, the cancer will grow,
so take off the starched shirt
and the glistening shoes. Bend down,
Grandfather, play with the damp haired boy.
It will help Father understand the belt
and your temper. For Uncle, retarded Uncle,
it is already too late. He cannot forget.
His brain is damaged. None of us can forget.

Aunts and uncles sit in pairs,
stiff backed couples with unsmiling children
around their feet. My sister says I am one
of those icy faces. It cannot be true,
for I would have leaned over to my cousin
and warned him of the war, the bullet.
I would never receive the postcard
telling me about sweat and heat,
the jungle filled with darkness.

I would see, standing next to Auntie,
the woman wearing the tight, green dress,
waiting to meet faithless Uncle
in the all-night diner on his Texas business trip.
I would chase her away. Cousin would
grow up with his father. Standing taut
at the foul line, Cousin would not turn,
eyes searching, frowning at school bleachers
where Auntie would sit alone.

Yet the face under my sister's fingertips
looks familiar. It is a thin, distant face,
and I would write a letter, a poem,
to the shadows in those eyes. I would
tell about life wandering away
down an avenue of years populated
with blind, groping ghosts.

I would write what I cannot speak,
for it is a scene both mine and not mine.
I place a sheet of paper in every hand,
but each related stranger gets up,
leaving an inky sheet on an empty chair.

Memory

Gathering wild day lily buds to stir fry,
to add gold light to bok choy's
crisp stems and veined leaves,
meadowed morning trails softly
from fingers soaked with dew.

For a moment, I remember
gentle, dead Uncle in another field
plucking blossoms to drop them
into the basket, stained
with black walnut oils,
on young Auntie's arm.
Near them, I see myself,
barefoot and unafraid,
watching their fingers touch
within silky, orange petals
flecked with rich pollen
shed from yellow stamens.

Red-winged blackbirds chatter
like raucous, carefree children,
winged, open mouths raised
from mullein stem perches.

I squint, quick and moist.
Slender, young Uncle
is gone.

Standing alone, I pause
feeling memory spiral upward
    and outward
like a breath exhaled to the sky.

I close my fist
on the powdery talcum
of pollen on my palms,

but the sunlight around me
only shimmers with dust.

Standing alone, I pause
feeling memory spiral upward
        and outward
like a breath exhaled to the sky.

I close my fist
on the powdery talcum
of pollen on my palms.

The sunlight around me
shimmers with dust.

Holding the Words

Old dreams return at odd moments
to flicker during sunlit hours
like finding a pearl button
in a lint-filled pocket.

An elevator door slides open,
and for a lingering moment
night shapes shimmer.

Words can do that.
White wine swirls
to remembered cadences

of the heart, flapping,
clothes-pinned on the line
and hung out to dry.

An aspen tree shivers
against a purple sky.
Ragged voices rage,

making ear drums quiver
with the rasped sound
of lung-wracked, disbelieving sobs.

And out of the darkness
(and would it be the same if it were light?),
come the words, like bits of broken glass,

bringing reflection's aching union
to unfinished images' tight embrace.

Inside the Poetry

The naming
and the sound of a thing
      were once one.
Words were not only words.

Syllables rooted like crescent seeds
with folded skin swollen
      in pulsing strength.

From the throat came silver,
wheat's thunder,
      and dawn's light.

Shaman chant recognized being
and captured its spinning,
      throbbing essence,
never stripping it
of flesh,
      strident song,
          or cascading soul.
The price was blood,
heart blood,
      menstrual blood,
          birthing blood
paid in kinship to needs
joined to nature's cycles.

Guidance

Yuan Mei found poetry waiting
    like fresh dew
on ordinary events.

Each poem exhaled images
    as natural
as tub water's receding sound.

Precise actions bore meaning,
    their present moments
speaking as her teacher.

She knew not to pound a garden path
    in heavy boots.
Gentle steps did not diminish.

A cup of steaming tea poured
    from a porcelain pot
clarified horizons of wild mountains.

Rinsing rice, slicing ginger and garlic,
and steaming fish were actions of history

grounded in an illumination of ancestors
suddenly awakened in living lines of poetry.

On Writing

It is the truth   certainly   entirely true
but I do not swear that the words
the beloved words
the cutting words
all these words which are my words
have any reality   perhaps no reality at all
in poetry
as in telling the truth
or in devising lies
when the words are free   having been carried
long enough on sagging shoulders
given away   thrust forth
they abandon the pen   learn to teach themselves
gather into themselves
their own lives   untouchable
much like a freshly remote yesterday
and more like a strangely familiar tomorrow

Moments

billowing silk dress
your hands and the wind
shy fumblers

mirrored, moon image...
your muscled shadow turns
at my silk robe opening

➡

my breasts rise. . .
offering you handfuls
of heartbeats

                  graveled breathing
                            softens as fingers loosen
                  the fist of damp sheets

➡

your sleeve corner
brushes the still trembling
tips of my nipples

                                    on your lips
                                    I bend to taste
                                    a wafer of moonlight

          my body   to yours
    impossible to tell   your breath
                    from mine

                              moonlight   across your skin
                                   damp sheets are luminous
                         our vows   light-locked

➡

fragrance of new pine
     off the hiking path
     you   tugging at my clothes

                                        viscous beat
                            the night rain drumming
                                     of your heart

                                              ➡

your fragrant scent
in my sleep   crackling fire
     along my spine

                              crimson salmon
                                roe heavy
                          leaps the fallen oak

➡

bat unwraps his wings
    cool air dries my breasts
        as you rise

                    silent, dawn flight
                    great blue heron   sky
                    the color of his wings

Tracks

Womanhood

The eggs, inner blossoms nestled deep
between the strength of my hipbones, are mine.
I hold them.   I hide the eggs.   I protect them.

Fertility is a secret seed nurtured through childhood,
sparkling through interior crevices and bends.
It is a throbbing fluid of ancestral rivers
and private streams held in by the circle's edge.

Desire drives the compulsion to look within
to see what I hold, but I close into myself.
Sustained by the circle, I encircle this time
of slim, individual growing and dreaming.

You bring what pulsates the tender membrane
of vernal eggs.   Awkward   strong   completion.

The binding circle of your arms sustains
itself within the physical sway of my curves,
and the point around which my world travels
shifts its axis with a ponderous swelling.

Changes are heavy within me.
I open my arms to share what is mine.
Like the spreading chestnut delivering
its fruit in season, the seed becomes
a rounded burr, splits wide,
and the richness within   slips free.

Choices

I know you are growing within me,
and I lay still in a transforming silence
like the soundlessness accompanying death.

The room is dark in these hours before dawn,
and quiet is an emptiness folding into the house.

There is a decision to be made here,
and from time to time, a soft heartbeat
I should not be able to hear brushes my ear.

Perhaps never being born bears
with it the echoes of immortality
without the experience of dying.

And still, I hear the rhythmic
pecking of a bird's small beak
against the walls of its closed box.

As I watch the sun rise in this room,
there is a sound like distant wings
high in the branches of a mountain pine.

This morning's sun has come
a long way to be born.

Nine Months

It is a labyrinth of stone
and I touch its honed coolness
with surety, for it is mine.
The sharp edges are difficult,
keen on tender fingertips,
but the warmth and the shadows
are from my blood, my heart.

There are no fortresses here,
no woven tapestries of guardians
or carved stone gargoyles of legend.
I stand barefoot, arms extended,
and marvel at the power of dreams
as rich as obsidian's black fire.

Every choice within the wild rock
has been a turning from the tight,
chaotic morass of sound.
I learn the importance of silence
first; the tiny sounds beckon
inward toward my own heartbeat.
I touch the feather of your breath.

Paths of Blood

When I am pregnant, my mother warns me
not to go to the house my husband is building

unless I am careful not to let the shadow
of his hammer fall upon me —

if I fail in this, my baby will be born
with a birthmark, and everyone will know.

In Mother's kitchen, I am told not to eat
duck, certain pieces of pig. Aunts argue

about whether I should eat watermelon.
My Irish husband is angry and then laughs.

As my pregnancy grows, aunts whisper
to Mother about the sweet, whiskeyed soup

she must make once the baby is born.
The ingredients begin to make me sweat.

I know I will have no choice but to eat it
and drink the teas Mother and Aunts will brew.

I vow to myself that I will not
fill my baby's life with strictures,

tap dances against disaster,
lists of *can nots* and *must nots*.

And yet when the new baby
lies sleeping in her crib,

I hear myself saying,
We can plan new bedrooms

to face the rising sun, so
northern oaks can protect them.

Not Nursing

Not despite infant, clenched fist protests
wailing forth with body clock regularity,
not despite drinking sips of ale,
and trying, trying not to be concerned,
tautly flooded with your gnawing hunger.
I ride the waves of want rippling
your tiny belly with insistent claws
and raking beneath the skin of my desire.
I unravel a thrashing need to feed you
while liquid swells within granite breasts.

I picture your head, dark damp hair,
emerging between my legs, and I feel
the warm flush of birthing liquid
wet between my upraised thighs.

I dream of snow-melt rushing
down swelling, flooding streams
on steep Sierra slopes.

I hear the rhythmic wash
of ocean's salt seasons
in hidden, damp sand coves.

Everything I touch
is wet with the scent
of mother's milk,

and still, the wail
of the need to be filled
and filled rocks and echoes.

I rage as my breasts' sap
hardens into a mute,
drumming ache.

I strip and pull, milking
thin whiteness from feverish,
swollen breasts. Aching

nipples tremble with
fluent, shriveling cries
pierced upon the depths

of my emptiness.

Two Left Paradise

How does a man tell a woman
that he, too, is tied to the earth?

No blood from the core
    of him to match
        the fullness of the moon.

No sheltering womb
    to swell with the passing
        of months, three times three.

No breasts to grow heavy
    with the thick richness
        and body warmth of milk.

But a man knows the rhythm
of the filled cradle rocking,

and his hands caress the sick child's
hot forehead, damp with fear.

He offers deep laughter to ripple
through the loving and the learning.

He, too, has bitten the sweet, white meat
of the ripe apple, crisp from autumn's tree,
and the juice has run, unbidden, down his chin.

Fruit

You stand, legs apart, yellow forsythia in bloom
behind you in the gusty spring yard of our first home.
Dark earth stains smear the shovel gripped
in leather-gloved hands.   Small trees
— nut, plum, cherry, apple — tightly burlapped,
stand by huge holes bottomed with rich compost,
awaiting young roots eager for watered fertility.
You bend, waiting for each tree to whisper,
 "fruit," into spring air fragrant with buds
and impossibly delicate sprays of blossoms.

Your Robert Frost proclivities, your Thoreau heart,
show through in gentle hands as you wind
protection around each tender trunk. You wrap
languid, clean layers, round and round, lapping
with care, to hold in life's sweet saps against
gnawing hungers and colorless, winter frosts.

And I, with your laughing baby on my hip,
watch your coaxing, tender love of soil and roots.
Your spell spreads, and the words rise
welling in my throat, *"fruit . . . fruit."*

Spring Planting With My Daughter

It nestled firmly in your hand
   as I brushed aside dry, oak leaves.
Humus was soft and moist,
   but the trowel shivered harshly in my hand.

The rock was blue black in its heaviness;
   no roots would ever pierce its unyielding bulk.
My searching trowel confirmed its unmoving presence.

I began to push the damp dirt
   back into that difficult hole,
   but I saw your small fingers
   tighten around the swelling daffodil bulb.
I heard myself say that spring
   would bring yellow petals of sunlight
   to greet you in the early morning.

Spring yellow to make you smile
   as you watched the flashing lights
   of the school bus stop.

I took off my dirt-stiff canvas gloves
   and began to feel for the edges of the rock
   with my groping fingertips.

Winged Kin

Through Irish lace curtains rippled by spring breezes,
I see her coming. Her capped head is bent low,

and her small hands cup a nest of dry grass
and tiny twigs. I wait for her on the porch,

listen to the frantic trickle of anxious sobbing.
My daughter and I bend our heads over an abandoned

nest cradling two, perfect, sky blue eggs
and the fragments of a third, broken, azure shell.

The nest sits on the railing as I hold my child tightly
until the crying softens. My fingertips cross the wet

silk of her cheeks. I rub morning sun into them . . .
and breezes soft as a damp moth's first breath.

I keep myself from speaking promises built on
a logic weaker than hot house flowers. I embrace

the wings, the wind, and the fall. I tuck the blue
cotton tail of her shirt into her denim jeans. I hold

the bent visor of her baseball cap as I touch
the brilliant blue eggshells she leaves behind.

I look up as she runs. My heart beats erratically
as I watch the wing-like sway of her flowing hair.

Taking Action

My son stands in childhood's light.
He calls me to the crown of thorns
branching its way up brown siding.
I nod and go to watch baby robins,
freshly feathered and nested
in pyracanthra's spiny twists.
I smile, recalling the day he found
broken blue shells and looked up
to see open mouths.

My son watched coarse, naked skin
become down and feathers. In the lid
of a mason jar, he placed freshly dug,
fleshy earthworms to be carried aloft
to insistent young. He counted
and frowned while five nestlings
slowly became two.

My son calls today, loudly.
His arms pull at air like a runner
caught in quicksand. Adult robins
dive, and dive again. I see a snake
winding its way up a branch, moving
closer to the nest, pausing only when
a winged parent hits its scaled body.

I am cold, still with pervasive order.
A child with fluttering fledglings
caught in the irises of his eyes turns
to see wings reflected in a snake's slit irises.
He does not accept an ordered universe,
a pattern of hollow gods and assigned truths.

➡

He grabs a muddy hoe and swings it
with a child's awkward force, swinging
four times, hitting the snake twice with its blade
before I stop him. I can feel language
and time spinning outward as I watch
the snake slide away from the nest,
slide down the house foundation,
slide into broken azalea branches
and moist roots mingled with flotsam
of leaf layer and damp humus.

My son stands grimly with the oversized hoe
tight in his grasp like a fierce sentinel.
With a sharp flutter of wings, two
baby robins move with small hops
onto thorned, outer branches.
Wings flap hard as each fledgling
flies a crooked pattern to land heavily
on our lawn's cedar, split-rail fence.

My son nods, throws aside his hoe,
and leans lightly against me as we watch
an adult robin, a grasshopper in its beak,
follow young robins into an arched canopy
of summer brambles and ripening berries.

Reflecting on Isaac's Mother

The Lord's request
brought Abraham and his son
to mountain heights.
They stood, alone,
with Abraham's conscience.

The boy's mother was not there.

She had not sharpened the knife
sheathed against Abraham's hip
or placed a final slice
of sweet bread in Isaac's hands.

It was a simple command from heaven
for the son's warm blood.
SACRIFICE HIM, no more.

His mother was not there
to give the howl of Clytemnestra
as Abraham's blade reflected sunlight.

No Old Testament poetic simplicity
could have softened her guttural growl
of bestial, incredulous defiance.

Father and son descended
from that lonely apex,
tested, full of perfect obedience.

As Abraham told his story,
did Sarah recall the blue weight
of a son damp with her waters

and the final flow of throbbing
blood to his curled body before
the cutting of the long, gray cord?

In the nights to come,
did her lips tremble and snarl
at the sound of Abraham's breath?

The Funeral of a Student

In watching grief ripple its greatness
across the mad rooftops of your mother's eyes,

I gathered to me the grammar of quiet words
and the vocabulary of mourning's ancient phrases.

I stopped as relatives and friends, tinctured
with the plenitude of loss, moved around us,
hushed by maternal suffering's opened heart.

I ached at the hammering disbelief
in your mother's hoarse whispers
that you, her first born, lay broken
upon the white silk of an oak coffin.

Wrapped in a fierce embrace,
we tried to put you back into that car,

breath into your lungs, familiar smile
onto your lips. We tried to hear hope

interlaced with a brilliant mind readied
for a moving string of tomorrows.

We tried to hold you there
long, long, to begin to let you go.

Dragon Water

Like the coiled, Asian dragon's
unseen, thick scale nipples,
it has become the custom
of women to hide the blood.

The brilliant pink becoming
a scarlet blossom is not
a topic to be mixed with
folded, white linen napkins.

A flushed reticence
envelopes the crimson
of blood's female rituals.

Womanhood's flow recedes
into secret, inner crevices
like the glacier lily, glimpsed
only in remote regions.

The blood sight becomes
the difficult stain
demeaned by sophisticated,
urban indifference.

Moon blood fades,
lost with the loss
of the ancient tribe's
thrumming, echoed call

➡

offered in celebration
of the girl child becoming
the blooded, fertile vessel
of tomorrow.

But still, the winged *lung*
unfolds its ponderous length
each spring to bear a mother's
moisture to the land, answering

the drumming
pulse of life's true beat,
following the darkening
trail of blood

toward the certitude,
the throbbing, wet center,
of a language flowing and
clotted with vermilion moonlight.

Entering Summer

Again, it is June.   The Great Swamp has shed spring's silken coolness
for a humid canopy of heat and bugs. Green algae and swamp cabbage

crowd open water, and white blossoms of wild rose scent the air.
Water parts soundlessly for gliding swans as their long necks bend

in hovering arcs over downy miniatures.   The crested plumage of preening
male wood duck brightens a marshy island. The cat tails part as his female

moves toward water's edge with a string of seven ducklings. In the distance,
tall trees hold huge, stick nests. Long-legged great blue heron fledglings stand

with heads cocked, beaks open, in beckoning need. Summer assembles.
Its haze of heat rises through stiff brambles like a stifling dream.

In the moment of a golden beak piercing green water,
before a heron lifts with the sound of liquid wind, a brilliance

wakens and shimmers, moving away as I hold my breath,
clench straining neck muscles, rise, and reach for it.

Meal for the Ancestors

Mother's hands place each porcelain bowl mounded with rice
around the embroidered ancestral dragon flexing its arched,
scaled tail across Grandmother's red silk tablecloth.

I bring out platters of sliced meat, filled dumplings,
and cut oranges. Incense sticks waft heavy scent
into every corner of the darkened room.

With gentle gracefulness, at ease with timeless customs,
Mother calls our dead, our ghostly familial backbone,
to a celebration meal of riches designed by centuries.

Honored ancestors must be informed. Like the glow
in a tiger's eye, the past is summoned to bask
in knowledge of a new marriage, promises of children.

This meal unites us. We bow three times
to silently milling generations called by undying
ties of blood to feast with the living.

All Mothers

Pulling the weeds near the spiky,
spreading vines of green tomato,
I move the thick stems and see
a grass-lined hollow, a soft nest
filled with brown, speckled eggs.
I look beyond the bristling zucchini plants
and through the staked snap peas to see
the fluttering wings of a mother quail.

I think of the nine months that you spent
fluttering and growing beneath my heart.
I remember the heavy weight of your coming
and the umbilical cord's sweet cutting,
never severing your link to my heart's blood.

I rise, knowing that in this year's garden,
there will be a wild place near unpicked tomatoes
where the weeds will grow thick and tall.

Generations

Mother's crescent-brimmed straw hat
with the wide, yellow satin ribbons
smells lightly of summer hay bales
as I swing its tea cup roundness
like a familiar fan across my face.

Sunlight is a flickering screen
of light and shadow unraveling
slowly against shifting breezes
as I move to the heavy shade
of the thickly leafed ash.

I sigh, leaning my elbows against
the white, wrought iron tabletop
as I reach into the deep, jade bowl.
My fingers encircle silken cream,
the cool skin of fresh picked apricots.

I hear again last night's quiet
softly broken by the gentle sound
of my parents, back from the city,
and carrying the unmoving, too still,
rice bag figure of Grandmother upstairs.

Inside, in the upstairs bedroom,
old Grandmother lies dreaming
her last dreams of cramped city rooms
filled with sweat scent heavy on
sleeping bodies of sprawled children

➡

or remembering the drifting dust
of a Canton village street waiting
to turn to thick, sucking mud
when summer skies flowed over
with lightning and monsoon days.

Heat lightning like a ragged weaving
of restless light appears above the trees.
A soft thunder rumbles its calm
exhalation like a candle's breath
across the sunlit luster of green lawn.

In the window, I see Mother look up
at summer clouds for ancient signs
of new weather, throbbing
with farewells, but pregnant
with clear, birthing waters.

Living Trail

From the Dead

I was young when Grandfather died
and the ride through the Holland Tunnel
was a silent one   no one shouted at the state line
in Chinatown a black band was tied to my arm
as I watched my father's shoulders   rise and fall
in an ancient grief   I did not then understand
my mother gave me candies   I sat in a wooden chair
rubbing my nose at the urgent smoke of incense   I wandered
looking into porcelain bowls filled with red envelopes
and not touching walls of flowers   stalks of gladiolus
stems of lilies and roses   red ribbons across each bunch
my brother was an infant   mostly sleeping
in my mother's arms   I rested my head
on her knees   and I was lifted into old auntie's lap
afraid   not knowing old auntie's face or touch
my cousin came and took my hand
old men nodded   cousin led me toward the door
and dollar bills were given to him along the way
outside   I clung in the daylight to cousin's hand
he knew his way through dirty, winding streets
crowded with boxes of vegetables   tubs of swimming fish
cooked chickens and ducks hanging with their heads down
in crisp skin death   he would stop to let me sip
my cold bottle of soda   at the noodle shop
I ate won ton from my soup with my chopsticks
and did not drink the broth   later we sat outside
eating roast pork buns   he talked to girls
who bent down and touched my hair
they wanted to pick me up   *he whispered let them*
and I'll take you to the park   I didn't
but he walked me over to the busy playground anyway
he pushed me on the swing a long time   back and forth

➡

I could taste the city dust as I swung   thinking about New Jersey
the family farm, my dog, the chickens white specks in the distant meadow
my swing visible to my mother from the kitchen window

I think now about the grandfather I did not know   I remember
my father's oldest sister leaning on his arm   grandmother silent
at the cemetery   my black suited father crying   his back stern and stiff
I remember later   how my father said that grandfather hit him
his brothers and sisters   I remember father saying
that's why I never hit you   and I remember now
the times my father would yell in anger   and never raise his hands.

I could taste the city dust as I swung   thinking about New Jersey
the family farm, my dog, the chickens white specks in the distant
meadow   my swing visible to my mother from the kitchen window

I think now about the grandfather I did not know   I remember
my father's oldest sister leaning on his arm   grandmother silent
at the cemetery my black suited father crying, his back stern and stiff
I remember later   how my father said that grandfather hit him
his brothers and sisters   I remember father saying
that's why I never hit you   and I remember now
the times my father would yell in anger   and never raised his hands.

Embracing Whole Days

Even when fists are full, overflowing with hours, days are
finite and piercingly brief. Light falters as the cooling marsh
receives back its ducks and geese after daylight hours spent
in corn fields and pastures. They return to sleep on open water.

Short eared owl crisscrosses open fields as the harrier's aerial
spirit feels the pull of twilight's throaty call across treetop roosts.
Bats flit overhead in a sky of spun ebony. Even when starlight
flickers like ancient, wet tears, I do not want to let the day depart.

The raccoon snuffling in my flashlight's beam lifts its head
and pauses before climbing up a shagbark hickory trunk,
crossing a moonlit, branched bridge to an oak's wide hole.

A great horned owl folds its wings and drops from the sky,
a winged arrow aimed toward rustling leaves. Later, vole bones
will fall into piles of droppings and fur bits near the big sycamore.

Moonlight parts grassy shadows, and the fox I had not seen until then
rises with disappointment, shakes its head, and slips back into the forest

before I can breathe again. A language I have come to learn slowly
beads its translated images across my skin with deepening dew.

Wind quickens, and sky's black vault is lit by the glint
upon Orion's shoulder and his hunting belt's triage fire.

The purity of night's muted dark and light makes these minutes
porous and calm. I can smell midnight's vapor settle around me.

Six deer trot across a rutted road and look back from beyond
wine berry thickets to watch me turn homeward, the full day in my arms.

As twigs snap beneath my feet, I hold hard to the day's thick bones,
sucking softly and swallowing the richness of its fatty marrow.

Absences

When old Poh Poh visits,
trailing the scent of Brooklyn streets,
we stand at the kitchen door
in welcome with our cheek's soft flesh
turned, vulnerable, to her thin lips.

When Poh Poh holds the stair railing
and warns, "Watch all steps.
All falls break bones. Remember,
remember old Aunty," we nod.

After all, old Aunty's bones
never healed before she died.
Sister tightens her firm grip
on Poh Poh's flowered dress.

I move slowly, two steps down
in front of Poh Poh's descending feet.
My hands reach up, and I say,
"Don't worry about falls. We're here."

But wherever my fingers reach,
there is air, empty air.
And I reach, thrashing,
into tomorrow's absent spaces

where old Aunty and Poh Poh,
free of wooden railings,
walk up stairs, smiling
and unafraid of falls.

Returning

I

It is a slow erasure. The diminished body lies
like an empty egg shell under white sheets. Shallow

breaths are accompanied by damp rattles and heavy
silences. The skin of her lips flake like dried petals.

Her married son and grown daughter have flown
across the United States to take turns in the long

death watch. Her sister, eighty years old, sits
by her side murmuring *"Catherine"* and rubbing

the tautly fissured veins of hands and arms bruised
black and blue. Shadowed blotches like dark oil

across white sand spill out from IV needles taped
to skin more translucent than a luna moth's wings.

II

Her ashes will be flown to California. A husband,
many years dead, waits beneath dry soil. Last night

she must have remembered him, recalled the babies,
relived the homemaking as her hands moved in air

to sew draperies, to hem and press dresses.
She must have turned on their heavy oak bed

to wrap arms around his shoulders, to taste
the gleam of moonlight on dreaming eyelids

➡

and chest hairs, softly curled like fiddlehead ferns.
Bright-eyed Caty must have been young again.

Today, medication's slow, intravenous drip
quiets the visible movement of ghosts,

but her mind remains distant with the scent
of starched shirts and the leap of children's laughter.

III

I listen to her silences, not yet like Father's last hours.
Breath's flutter has the wing song of a trapped sparrow.

"Are you comfortable?" *"Any pain?"* still has meaning.
Ministrations of shifted body and tubes of oxygen

follow along wrinkles and joints to travel the body's
belief in itself, the familiar grip of continued presence.

The dark, soft language of erasure, the sweep of present
time and future time into the chalky dust of past time

has yet to come. The tight, steady flap of wings waits
to glide soundlessly into opened seams of night.

Lessons

I

The vole, bent awkwardly between the claws
of the neighbor's cat, shakes without pride.
The silent vole flails when even to breathe
bleeds its pulsating pain across feline fur.

The golden cat lifts its head in preoccupied ease
without moving body or extended paw.
I recall yesterday as a laxly muscled,
purring bundle was carried to the family car
in a child's brusquely affectionate arms.

I feel the vole's heart caving in, but the claws
fully contain its thrashing. I approach
as the cat lays back its ears. I watch cat fur
momentarily rise and fall back as I pause.

For a long moment, my will urges the kill. I wish
the vole its moment of death. But the cat waits,
waits past the time of reason into the pause of pleasure,
and anger's bile fills my mouth. Muscles taut,
I lift my book to heave it at the cat.

There is a tiny eruption of blood as clawed knives
slash the vole's body while its dripping, spastic limbs
are tossed into the air. The broken ruin lands
at my feet as I shudder and jump back.

With no acknowledgement of reason or emotion,
the cat picks up the supple flesh and turns for home.

➡

II

I let go of dreams in the shower's steaming heat.
In front of an unscreened expanse of kitchen window,
I coax thoughts of the day's routine into the perspective
of downy woodpecker's rhythmic pecking on seeded suet.
I watch finches flutter over the bit of fur and broken skull
under the crabapple tree. Those remnants like the wrinkled,
scattered petals of roses too long past their time of blooming
are all that remains of yesterday's vole. One finch lands
and pecks at the fur. Feathered head tilts before picking up
a broken piece of bone. With a lift of wings, it drops
the small, finished splendor of vole spirit.
I rise and press my hands against glass to see
if there is a pattern of boundaries, a message
of infinity, left in the air between the departing finch
and the scattered design of vole intentions.

III

Sunset shadows deepen like an arc of darkness
spreading its blinding sheen across vision's depth.
Perspectives shift from black ebony to soft pewter
in the thin light of a rising, ancient moon.
Night's texture is given spreading substance
by horned owl's throaty voice. I follow
its call into the woods to the base of a tree
that fingertips remember as a shagbark hickory.
In the amplified clarity of silence, I sense
the tufted, shadow form in the trunk's cleft.
A white throat shimmers in the slow movement
of rotated head, and I hold my breath.
The owl's yellow eyes are open like a child's eyes
struck with wonder, senses filled with hunger.
Its eyes meet mine, and I strive to memorize
how the moon dilates over its liquid surface,
how the moon glows with a cat's feral vision.

Graves

When my father turned to me, I didn't expect
to hear about their cemetery lots.   *"Hill top . . .
with a view."* He spoke as if he were describing
prime real estate, the building lot a dreamer
buys for his bride while planning picture windows
and numbers of bathrooms and nurseries.

"We won't be lonely." A litany
of neighbors, familiar names,
claim nearby premium lots.
And for family, who wish
to join my father and mother,
extra sites have been purchased.

"Morning sun . . . and trees." In a voice
of expectancy, stirred by details
influencing their choice, reflecting
good family luck and wisdom,
my father is asking for my approval.

My grandfather's grave is in Brooklyn,
and I remember flowers planted by his stone.
One grandmother lies in Canton, and she never
saw her daughter's children. I have
not seen her grave, but I have imagined
its small bulk and carved Chinese characters.

I remember eating roast pork buns
at the Brooklyn cemetery, watching
my father fill a bucket at a wall spigot
to water trees near Grandfather's grave.

➤

Grandmother and Mother walked
grassy cemetery rows reading aloud
names and dates. I ran my finger in
the cold crevices of tombstone words.
Grief held no body, no reality then.

But today, as I watch my father's
thin legs tremble, I know
his coffin, without windows,
cannot long remain empty.

A sparrow hovers and lands
on the porch railing as I begin
to speak about the beauty
of wind, sun, and hill top views.

Dignity

Resting in a worn oak chair, pillows
propped against the small of his back,
Father's death illness reflects into the room
through the quiet eyes of his grandchildren.
Against the blanket upon Father's knees,
one grandchild rests a bent head
while another sleeps, not upon
Father's lap, but stretched across
the carpet at his unmoving feet.

Father is awake in twilight's
moving light. Evening works its way
across browned tomato vines.
Cooling air fills with the distant,
roosting cries of wild turkeys.

Through the darkening room's open window,
Father's eyes rest a long time upon my brother,
tall doctor smoking by Mother's rose bushes.
Father watches the cigarette tip brighten and glow
in a night beginning to fill with stars.

The past opens to press against his silence.
And for a moment, there is a scent like fresh hay
and a younger Father paces beside a cow,
huge with calf and bellowing in her labor.
He runs his hands hard along her side, grunting
in sympathy with the rippling twitches of her flesh.
In satisfaction, he watches the wetly folded calf
flow and fall from her. His hands already reach
to clear its face and breathing passages.
As that long ago calf rises on damp legs
seeking its mother's heavy udders, Father
rubs its sides with straw and laughs.

In today's deepening shadow,
Father reaches down to stroke
the blackness of his grandchild's hair.
A bright leaf of memory turns in his eyes.
He smiles before he coughs and turns
his head, so I can no longer see his face.

Long Illness

Maybe dreams of death always precede death.
In the light air of dreams, the living hand
has already slipped itself into death's firm grip.
Inside the dream, the first steps in the long exile
from life are taken with a firmness like stepping
out onto a receding wave, not sinking, but walking
outward on water in rhythm with the natural tide.
Along the darkening edges, there is the sense
of something coming, a seminal sound that rises
like a familiar note sometimes heard in prayers.
The continuous connections to flesh, to the scent
of sweat and the taste of love, these are stretched
thin as heart sound vibrating faintly on eardrums.
Perhaps within dreams, there is the purposeful
surrender of the slender, glacier lily
to the sheltering cold of winter.

Sitting long hours with my frail mother
by my father's bedside, I feel
my breath become light as his, thin
as snow-melt trickling across gray ice.
I hear my voice flutter and murmur,
Dream now, for Mother's sake, dream
and know she held your hand
to the very end and never let go.

Family

All afternoon the ox tail soup simmered on the stove,
bubbling with the meaty fragrance of a winter soup.

My mother said that goodness lay in its ability
to thicken blood, to produce a spreading redness

like dragon's blood sedum. When wind blew rain
sparkling with bits of hard ice against the window,

we sank into the moist warmth of Mother's kitchen.
Our rice bowls filled, steaming with heart's medicine.

Recipes, generations old, mixed with the sizzle of family,
simmered beliefs that crossed an ocean without losing the kiss

of Grandmother's voice. Blended with the flavor of ginger
and garlic, the salt of tears steamed its strength into broth

offered with the caress of a hand upon an upraised face.
I did not know to savor that moment's wholeness,

to watch my brothers sucking on dripping bones
while little sister added chopped scallions to her rice

and Father spooned a single mouthful from the pot
before adding more pepper. I should have eaten more

while snow became ice formed like petals of white
chrysanthemums falling in total silence from the sky.

As Mother is helped to lay white chrysanthemums
upon Father's fresh grave, I swallow hard

to remember, to move past a gnawing hunger,
to lean my back against that stove's warmth once again.

Lineage

Mother's scrapbook holds frozen reflections,
time markers on a liquid stream of family events.
Grandfather, long dead, stares back with a careless
glance like Li-Po upon seeing a passing peasant
badly mounted on a stiff-legged, tired horse.
Father looks at me from a slender, boyish body
that seems to move with the grace of my brothers
and the childish wonder of my young son.
Mother, her hair done like a movie star, sits
on a blanket spread on a sunny Long Island beach.

I know she gets cold so easily. The setting red
of that long ago sun must bring Father's jacket
to her shoulders. She is only twenty.
I think even then she must have a basket,
carefully packed, filled with roast pork,
sauced and sliced as he likes best.

We sit with our heads close together today,
and she tells me the arthritis in her fingers hurts.
She softly tugs Father's old sweater around
her shoulders and frees another photograph
from its glued corners for me to take home.

Softly Aging

When a woman stands within her fourth decade,
different rooms begin to beckon.

Going by bronze-framed
photographs stirs whispers
as ears strain to hear sounds
like snowflakes hitting
darkened window panes.

The air is still within this house
where I sit and hear horned owl's call
even through closed windows.

The tea kettle whistles with swollen heat,
and words I write rise like steam
above the fragrant oils of my bath.

The mirror is damp with moisture,
and the towel squeaks against its surface;
my silent reflection remains streaked.

Wrapped in damp towels, I walk
down hallways, softly lit,
and past doors quietly, firmly shut.

I do not knock.

I know this is my house,
and I am not afraid.

It is just some doors
are not meant
to be re-opened.

Understanding

Already round buds of peonies weigh down tall stems.
Each closed life bends to touch brown earth before cracking

into a moon form bursting toward fullness in layers
of unfolding petals. Impossibly huge blossoms

grace thick bushes covering slopes around a cedar porch.
Nature strews snowy petals. Her abundance brings bees

and ants swarming in hunger's unrelenting pull.
Wings and legs drive lust into pollen's thick powder.

There is no time for questions. The importance of life
manifests itself in action. Burgeoning vitality flares

upon an inner silk of death. Absence now would be
desertion. Dreams of passion, real or unreal, exist

in this moment. Today's ecstasy of fulfillment throbs
against the richness of a white flowered slope. It is a light

like love, and its hunger is our truth. The present
is iridescent. It is enough to know tomorrow holds

death's inevitability. Illuminated air vibrates
with nature's scent of blooming. I shake

a dancing ant from a petal's lip before I clip
a single blossom to place next to your wine glass.

Payment

I

As ice forms and thickens on juniper needles,
green branches against winter's bared sinew slopes
sag to bend toward wind drifts of snow.

Debts are like that. The deepest debt forms,
soundless and transparent, around a raised spirit.
With time's passage, the chill of seasons,

a perceptible droop develops like a small grief.
As winds grip, a demand for payment
swirls and thickens around feet and legs.

The shadow lifts its face from stone and stretches
while I strain in this brittle light to see if it is your form,
the translucent, folded shape you had before dying.

Do I acknowledge all I have been bequeathed from the whetted,
double edge of custom offered like a foothold, the first slippage
on a path resistant to claw marks scripted across granular ice?

If the debt is genuine, I can never finish paying.

II

The shadow grows in silence like an open
doorway, coalesces and rises against the silver
of my sight. I begin to believe I hear the dead

speaking of ancestral sacrifices owned across generations
while practiced payments wither in my hands. My blood
account comes due with a cry like a young seal cut

from the herd by a white shark. And like the foundering
seal, I lift my head once, eyes wide, heart pounding with
understanding, before slipping into sparkling

flakes of timelessness. Memory knows the fresh shape
rising, forming, from time's bright roots, struggling
to define the surface it splinters and absorbs. I recognize

a familiar turn of head and know with icy certitude
that the only visible shadow is my own, its dark center,
an indentured substance pulsing with inherited flickers of light.

Blood Trail

I

Watery distance with surf pounding
in our ears is where we come from.
Through a dark that becomes light
we drift to cyclic rhythms
like spring rain's rich drumming,
calling for blood, calling for blossom.

Bones fold and fingers grasp
as the womb's small tide pool
breaks free to join an ocean
of cloudless air.

Not a boy this time. You can try again.

II

Words on our tongues glisten
in the learning. On some lips,
the burden blazes to leave wounds.
A frail web, spun of gossamer lullabies
and innocent laughter, forms a dry,
itching scab to hold in the blood.

For the first time, always the first time,
beauty flares and pain shadows
without justification. The dream opens
and closes like a growing sea anemone
to the throes of a changing tide
of water too bright for drowning.

Which language, which one should I speak?

III

Like the sound of a horned owl's wings
in a night filled with crickets drawing
grief across the veins of their thighs,
the web's humming leads everywhere
before dissolving into the flutter
of midnight's luna moth

Upon learning the language of rain,
the taste of its blood fills our mouths.
Teach us to breathe again in water.
Wash each scar until the crusty lichen
breaks through bedrock to free the alpine lily.

Understand this. Father grappled like a defiant
Sung warrior against the squatting dragon of death.

➡

IV

We leave tracks across a salt marsh
teeming with life. Swamp cabbage
and wild garlic scents fill the air.
Yellow bladderwort thrusts its gold
upon dark water alive with dragonflies.
Harriers crisscross an open sky.

The milt of dreams hangs in watery depths
like abundant algae moving to settle
on a mud-sand bottom. We leave
tracks like wounds on living water.
We leave marks of passing like great,
flat flowers of rose mallow
placed for others to follow.

My daughter and son . . . the first grandchildren.

V

On one leg, its head tucked beneath
feathers the color of snow, the egret
sleeps while the stars on Orion's belt
are the eyes, the tongue, and the feet
leading the way over granite mountains.

A rain-soaked veil of clouds
passes over the white glow
of the moon freeing itself
from an oak limb's stiff grasp.

On droplets of bird song,
a fugue that follows the soul
like an earnest shadow rises.
A shapelessness we find familiar
approaches, and we move forward
knowing the throbbing kinship
of lightning and thunder, moon and earth,
and rivers and oceans and blood.

Fortune

I

Lighting firecrackers in China chased away evil spirits.
But in Grandfather's village on the Pearl River delta, loud crashes

did not dismiss.   Fiery noise summoned good fortune.
Fortune's loud call might bring fish to steam with scallion and ginger

and eggs, big hens' eggs, to salt. The cascading of currents,
water tones wild as lover's hair across a bare chest,

would be fluid music, nature's own drum, to summon dragons
with spring rain under their wings to make rice grow.

Villagers' stomachs would roar in old China when thunder,
the call of winged lizards, echoed across gray skies. Wives

would cover their heads with baskets while watching
through sheets of rain for a glimpse of fiery eyes,

a winged lord to ask for children, armfuls of children.
Fortune reflected in the continued spin of life's cycles.

II

Fortune is a dark presence that travels along grief's electricity
at Father's funeral.   Mother stands in a veil of exhaustion,

leaning heavily on Auntie's arm.   Grief's hollow center is pierced
by brother's sobs, sharp as a cicada's shrill, long as the sucking dry

➡

of a raw egg. The thunder of life is muted, but fortune's echo lingers
like wheels ringing on a worn road. We witness its consolation

faintly warring with the first shovelful of dirt. My feet are rooted
to the earth, set into the dried mud of an ancient stream. Each

word in my mind is a fragment of broken sound as I grasp
the hands of my daughter. My husband lifted Father's thin frame

that last morning. My son remembers his grandfather's last breath.
The pure white of Mother's hair trembles like a crane's feathers

in a damp wind as the labyrinth of a life widens and fades
like freshly pruned branches opening to reveal a skyward space.

Florence McGinn is the Senior Executive Vice President for Global Knowledge Exchange and the CEO of Insynthesis, an educational and writing consultancy. She is a former United States Commissioner on the Clinton administration's Web-based Education Commission, where she chaired National K-12 Issues. She was United States National Technology and Learning Teacher of the Year in 1998. She has received Princeton University's Distinguished Secondary School Educator award, the United States Eastern Region Teacher of the Year award, the New Jersey Teacher of the Year award, and several Best Educational Practices awards. She serves on the Board of Trustees of GKE Foundation and Mediatech Foundation as well as on the advisory boards of Cisco Learning Institute, SchoolTone Alliance, PBS OnLine, and *Technology and Learning* magazine. Florence McGinn has keynoted and presented on technology-assisted learning and provided educational advocacy throughout the United States as well as in Australia, Singapore, Japan, China, Italy, and Korea.

Florence McGinn has published poetry widely in journals that include *Midwest Poetry Review, Modern Haiku, Voices International,* and *Parnassus.* She has published children's poetry in *Cricket* and *Clubhouse.* One of her children's poems is utilized by McGraw-Hill in its standardized tests. Another poem won a Peet's Coffee Poetry Prize in California and was utilized for advertising. Mrs. McGinn has held an appointment as Off-Campus Poetry Professor to Dianye School in Beijing, China. CD-ROMs on "Educational Digital Velocity" that feature Mrs. McGinn's innovative educational methodologies are published in China by Shanghai-based Centrix Technology, Nankai University, and GKE. Her essays, articles, and educational support materials have been published by agencies such as PBS, the Milken Foundation, Singapore's *School and Curriculum Journal, Media and Methods,* the Asia Media and Information Center, Amnesty International, and AT&T. Additionally, Mrs. McGinn's educator materials are published online in alignment with China's National English Language textbook and GKE's Professional QUEST Development materials. Mrs. McGinn has over 20 years of classroom experience, has designed and taught innovative English, creative writing, and emerging technologies courses, taught on technology-assisted learning in New Jersey Educational Teacher Training Centers as well as in a televised, ten part series produced by NJ Network.

Publisher's Note

PENNYWHISTLE PRESS CELEBRATES THE MILLENNIUM!

Established in 1986 the Press has grown, maintaining a lively conversation between the authors it has published and their readers as it hopes to continue relating to and with the poets, writers, critics, reviewers and readers of the future.

The Press has expanded its outreach and its books are distributed by Small Press Distribution of Emeryville, California and various other distributors and wholesalers.

The publication of **Bosque Redondo: The Enchanted Grove** by *Keith Wilson,* features another noteworthy poet whose distinguished voice reaches out to all. The concurrent publication of **Blood Trail** by *Florence McGinn* marks the 31st title in its Poetry series.

Pennywhistle's latest collection of distinguished and important poetry underlines the commitment the Press has made to share a wide range of voices, presented in a responsible manner to a public seriously interested in good work and an expansion of the landscape of poetry.

The Press currently offers the following titles in its Chapbook Series:

The Blue Series

Sublunary

Jorge H, -Aigla's writing goes to the heart of experience with clarity, illuminating truth as perceived by him. Taking his cues from the dark side of life, *Aigla* reaches out with caring insight..

32 pages $6.00, ISBN 0-938631-07-1

Full Turn

Sarah Blake's book exposes the sacred territory of domestic blood connections, of love and family–demonstrating how ordinary life has a tendency to trap and bind. *Blake* roots herself in the present and struggles with ghosts of the past, convincingly adept at being both here and there at once.

32 pages $6.00, ISBN 0-938631-08-X

Further Sightings & Conversations

Jerome Rothenberg has an overriding preoccupation with seeing. His work comes from a need for concentrated visionary representation. Shaman and High Priest of language, he sings as he explores and blesses the world.

32 pages $6.00, ISBN 0-938631-03-9

The Fields

Richard Silberg's work is spare and complicated and speaks to the process of personal discovery. His brilliant resolutions bring one home.

32 pages $6.00, ISBN 0-938631-05-5

Who is Alice?

Phyllis Stowell's preoccupation with the need for a common language between the sexes generates a passionately argued sequence of poems about silence.

32 pages $6.00, ISBN 0-938631-04-7

The Sum Complexities of the Humble Field

Viola Weinberg offers a poetry of the sensual that can be tasted and touched. At the same time, she presents her world with discipline and mathematical precision.

32 pages $6.00, ISBN 0-938631-06-3

The Red Series

No Golden Gate for Us

Francisco X. Alarcon's poems give simultaneous voice to the pain and humor of the desperado who has seen and felt too much and to the quiet understanding that comes with wisdom.

32 pages $6.00, ISBN 0-938631-16-0

Tesuque Poems

Victor di Suvero embraces a world grounded in arroyos and trees, lightning storms and streams. Complicated and thought-provoking, his poetry celebrates survival while praising the phenomena of existence.

32 pages $6.00, ISBN 0-938631-17-9

Hardwired for Love

Judyth Hill takes her readers on a lyrical roller coaster ride through ancient past toward a luminous future. Her essential message is direct, and her laughter, sensuality, intelligence and exuberance infuses her work with love, spiritual awareness and aesthetic discipline.

32 pages $6.00, ISBN 0-938631-13-6

The Width of a Vibrato

Edith A. Jenkins writes a poetry of affirmation that begins with awareness of loss and is dwelt upon until the poet is able to transmute that loss into affirmation.

32 pages $6.00, ISBN 0-938631-10-1

Portal

Joyce Jenkins poetry offers readers a rare combination of playfulness spoken with wisdom–showing a complex nature devoid of bitterness.

32 pages $6.00, ISBN 0-938631-18-7

Falling Short of Heaven

Susan Lummis' work is the quintessence of a high strung, highly sensitive and wildly intelligent woman's attempt to get along in this big, bad world. Her poetry is written with a theatrical feel that makes it seem lived in.

32 pages $6.00, ISBN 0-938631-12-8

ρ

The Green Series

Where you've Seen Her

Grace Bauer has earned her reputation for a clear and incisive use of language. *Ms. Bauer* illuminates her subject matter with an honesty all too rare in today's world.

32 pages $6.00, ISBN 0-938631-11-X

Decoy's Desire

Kerry Shawn Keys' appreciation of the natural beauty of his world–specifically that lush hillside in Perry Co., Pennsylvania–surfaces throughout this collection.

32 pages $6.00, ISBN 0-938631-14-4

What Makes a Woman Beautiful

Joan Logghe shares a voice as ancient and wise as time. With gleaming syntax honed to perfection, *Ms. Logghe's* women–and men–live their everyday realities and how "beauty" abides and sustains.

32 pages $6.00, ISBN 0-938631-15-2

Chaos Comics

Jack Marshall's work is sensual and intense; his supple, possibilities of perception with a philosophy that is breathtaking in its audacity and scope.

32 pages $6.00, ISBN 0-938631-25-X

Between Landscapes

Wai-Lim Yip has created a magical, musical scale that enchants, soothes and lulls, rises and falls, as it simultaneously plunges us into the beauty and power of the terrible and sublime cycles of nature.

32 pages $6.00, ISBN 0-938631-24-1

Sextet One

The first anthology in Pennywhistle's new series. This volume presents the work of six separate and distinct poets with each presentation containing an introduction by a noted critic or poet, a photo of the author and a collection of the poet's most recent work–a wonderful way to bring six new friends into one's life! This volume presents *Kim Addonizio, Tom Fitzsimmons, Harry Lawton, Annamaria Napolitano, Doren Robbins and Ruth Stone, with introductions by Dorianne Laux, Victor di Suvero, Maurya Simon, Pierre Saint-Amand, Philip Levine and Rebecca Seiferle.*

226 pages $17.50, ISBN 0-938631-27-6

In the paperback full volume Poetry Series it offers it's latest publications as stated above.

ρ

Bosque Redondo

Is a moving collection of poems whose theme is the evocative power of memory. In the hands of the poet memory becomes the catharsis that opens up the world of childhood, a space the poet must revisit. Noted voice of the Post Beat era, *Keith Wilson*, friend of *Charles Olson, Sid Corman, Robert Duncan, Robert Creeley and Gary Snyder*, recognized the responsible voice of his time in New Mexico and in the West.

108 pages $12.00, ISBN 0-938631-35-7

Blood Trail

The cross-cultural currents that have enriched American writing in the later part of the 20th century continue to be part of the literary scene today. *Florence McGinn's* work continues that cross-cultural adventure. Her poetry, crafted with care for the detail of her Chinese heritage, reaches into our consciousness with current American scenes and with language that touches our hearts.

108 pages $12.00, ISBN 0-938631-34-9

naked Heart

This collection of *Victor di Suvero's* as poetry is a compendium of poems which dance between the wise old street experiences of San Francisco to the delicate and sensual places we learn to honor through love and time. This selection makes the case for love exciting, erotic, evocative and thoughtful...all at the sam*e time. Poet James Broughton says that, "di Suvero is valiant to take the risk of disrobing his heart— it's the only way to be a genuine poet."* And poet and Nuyorican Cafe founder, *Bob Holman,* has this to say: *"When you listen to the beat of di Suvero's collection, **naked Heart,** you will hear yourself falling in love with poetry."*

80 pages $12.00, ISBN 0-938631-28-4

Hooplas!

Is a collection of festive tributes to friends and intimates of the author, who salutes their talents and personalities with song, fanfare and wit. These odes for odd occasions are offered in praise of friendship, in memory of merriment, and in awe of love. The poet died in 1999 best left this special tribute to his many friends.

93 pages $8.95, ISBN 0-938631-02-0

ρ

In the Anthology Series it offers the following:

¡Saludos!

¡Saludos! **Poemas de Nuevo Mexico** is the first bilingual anthology of the poetry of New Mexico. Sixty six fine Native American, Hispanic and Anglo poets share their experience of the Land of Enchantment with clear and heartfelt poems that sing! Poets represented in this strong and unique collection include *Miriam Sagan, Jim Sage, Leo Romero, Charles Bell, Greg Glazner, Peggy Pond Church, Luci Tapahonso and Joy Harjo,* among others.

290 pages $15.00, ISBN 0-938631-33-0

Voces del Rincon/Voices from the Corner

A collection of the poetic personae of *Michael Sutin* addressing issues pertinent to life lived in the corners of the New Mexico landscape crossed by the network of the highways of today.

180 pages $15.00, ISBN 0-938631-37-3

Ordering Information

Call your order to 505-982-0066
or fax it to 505-982-6858

ℓ
or write to
PENNYWHISTLE PRESS
Post Office Box 734
Tesuque, New Mexico 87574